September
Patterns & Projects

Newbridge Educational Publishing, LLC
New York

The purchase of this book entitles the buyer to duplicate
these pages for use by students in the buyer's classroom.
All other permissions must be obtained from the publisher.

ISBN: 1-58273-125-X

10 9 8 7 6 5 4 3 2

Table of Contents

Table of Contents (Continued)

ANIMAL ACTIVITY CENTERS

You need:
• crayons or markers
• glue
• oaktag
• scissors
• tape or stapler

1. Reproduce all the animal patterns on pages 7, 9, and 11. Color, mount on oaktag, and cut out.
2. Attach each activity center sign to a wall or a bulletin board in a different area of the classroom.
3. For the Rabbit's Reading Center on pages 6 and 7, assemble such supplies as: rugs, pillows, cushions, table with writing supplies, old typewriter, computer, tape recorder and record player, earphones, and books obtained from donations, garage sales, public library. If possible, place an empty baby pool in the reading corner and fill it with pillows and cushions. For activities, see Rabbit's Reading Center and Class Books on page 6.
4. For the Snake's Science Center on pages 8 and 9, assemble such supplies as: measuring sticks, cups, spoons, balance scale, sand and water table, aquarium with fish or lizards, live plants, small animals in cages, magnifying glass, magnets, empty jars, bags and boxes to fill with collections, old nature magazines, reference books, and collections of rocks, shells, bones, and leaves. For activities, see Magnet Mania and Looking at Leaves on page 8.
5. For the Armadillo's Art Center on pages 10 and 11, assemble such supplies as: easel, old shower curtains and tablecloths to catch drips, newspapers, a variety of paints, brushes, craft dough, rollers, cookie cutters, collections of scraps, old magazines for cutting, stamp pads and stamps, markers, crayons, colored chalk, and scissors. For activities, see Armadillo's Art Center Fun and Finish the Pictures on page 10.
6. Send home a list of items needed for the centers at the beginning of the year. Be sure to include storage containers such as oatmeal boxes and margarine tubs on the list.

RABBIT'S READING CENTER

1. Read a book from the reading center to the class.
2. Have children illustrate their favorite parts of the story.
3. Encourage each child to write or dictate a sentence about why he or she enjoyed the book.
4. Have children show their pictures in front of the class. Help them read the "book reviews."
5. Display the book reviews around the center.

CLASS BOOKS

You need:
• crayons or markers
• construction paper
• hole puncher
• pipe cleaners

1. Ask each child to contribute a page to the class book by drawing a picture on construction paper about something to do with fall, such as leaves changing color, children returning to school, and so on.
2. Have children write or dictate sentences about their pictures.
3. Stack all the pictures together. Punch three holes along the left sides of the pictures, as shown.
4. Add a title page to the front of the book.
5. Thread a pipe cleaner through each set of holes in the pictures. Twist the pipe cleaners to fasten.
6. After reading the book aloud to the class, place the book in the reading center for children to enjoy. Encourage children to work together in groups to make other books for the reading center.

Rabbit's Reading Center Pattern

READ

SNAKE'S SCIENCE CENTER—MAGNET MANIA

1. Lay out an assortment of both metal and nonmetal objects on a table in the science center.
2. Provide children with a horseshoe magnet and a bar magnet.
3. Ask children to sort into piles things that the magnets attract and things that the magnets do not attract.
4. Ask children to think about and try to explain why magnets attract some things and why they don't attract others.
5. Provide time for further experimentation and encourage children to test if magnets can attract metal objects through water, cloth, and paper.

LOOKING AT LEAVES

1. Lay out an assortment of leaves on a table in the science center.
2. Encourage children to feel the leaves and examine them through a magnifying glass.
3. Show children how to make leaf rubbings by placing a leaf under a piece of paper and rubbing the side of a crayon over the paper.
4. Help children search through books about leaves to identify the trees from which the leaves fell.
5. Ask children to group similarly shaped leaves together.
6. Ask children to close their eyes and try to identify similar leaves by the way they feel.

Snake's Science Center Pattern

ARMADILLO'S ART CENTER FUN

You need:
• hole puncher
• construction paper
• crayons or markers
• margarine container
• glue

 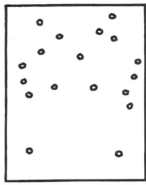 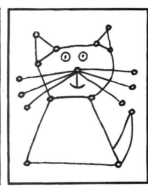

1. Show children how to use a hole puncher to randomly punch holes in construction paper.
2. Ask each child to connect the holes to make a design by drawing lines between them with a crayon.
3. Tell children to think about what their designs resemble. Have children add details to complete their drawings.
4. Ask children to gather the tiny circles they punched out of the construction paper and put them in a margarine container. Children may choose different-colored circles to glue onto their drawings to make mosaic patterns.
5. Display the pictures in the art center.

FINISH THE PICTURES

You need:
• old magazines
• scissors
• glue
• drawing paper
• crayons or markers

1. Find twenty large pictures of objects familiar to children in old magazines and cut them out.
2. Cut each picture in half and glue one half onto a piece of drawing paper. (Discard the other half of each picture.)
3. Place the pictures in the art center. During free time, let children draw in the other halves of the pictures.

GRANDPARENT'S DAY CARDS

Help children make cards to give on Grandparent's Day, the second Sunday in September.

You need:
• crayons or markers
• scissors
• construction paper
• glue
• stapler

1. Reproduce the card on page 13 for each child. Have children color the cards and cut them out.
2. Hold a discussion with children about activities they have shared with their grandparents. If some children do not have grandparents, ask children to think of some things they might enjoy doing with an older person, such as going to a movie, reading stories, taking walks, or going shopping.
3. Help children trace the cards on two pieces of construction paper and cut out.
4. Have children mount the cards on the first piece of construction paper.
5. On the other piece of construction paper, ask each child to draw a picture of himself or herself with a grandparent or an older person. Children may draw a picture of something that they have already experienced, or they may invent interesting adventures with grandparents or older friends.
6. Have each child write or dictate a sentence about the illustration and sign the card.
7. Staple the card together along the left side.
8. Have children bring the cards home to give or send to their grandparents or other older people who are special to them on Grandparent's Day.

ADOPTING GRANDPARENTS

1. Many residents of retirement homes do not have family members nearby. Some might welcome their "adoption" as grandparents by a class of young children. Check with the director of the facility as well as school officials before planning a visit.
2. Children may make cards and bring them to a retirement home or a senior citizen activity center when they visit.
3. Activities with a group of senior citizens can be planned for the enjoyment of both the children and the older people, such as art activities, making cookies, playing board games, or singing.
4. Children can write or dictate letters to their adopted grandparents throughout the school year.

Grandparent's Day Card

With
X
X
O
X
O

GRANDPARENT'S DAY BOOKMARKS

You need:
- crayons or markers
- glue
- oaktag
- scissors
- glitter, fabric strips, and foil

1. Reproduce the page of bookmarks on page 15 for each child. Have children color the bookmarks, mount on oaktag, and cut out.
2. Let children decorate the bookmarks with glitter, fabric strips, foil, and so on.
3. Children can write or dictate a short special message to grandparents or other older friends on the backs of the bookmarks.

14

Grandparent's Day Bookmarks

GRANDPARENT'S DAY VASE AND FLOWERS

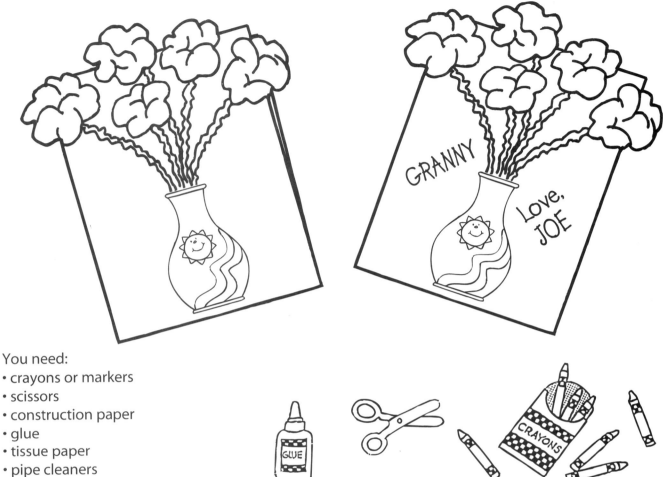

You need:
- crayons or markers
- scissors
- construction paper
- glue
- tissue paper
- pipe cleaners
- stapler

1. Reproduce the vase pattern on page 17 for each child. Have children color the vases and cut out.
2. Show each child how to position his or her vase close to the bottom of a sheet of construction paper. Have each child glue around the edges of the vase, leaving the top open.
3. Give each child several pipe cleaners to glue inside the vases, as shown.
4. Show children how to crumple squares of tissue paper and twist them around the pipe cleaner flower stems. Staple in place, as shown.

Alternate Activity

1. Take the class on a nature walk, pointing out signs of fall.
2. Have children gather dried grasses, leaves, and weeds on their walk. Use a grocery bag to collect the nature items.
3. After returning to the classroom, give each child a handful of nature items.
4. Have children arrange their nature items in their vases, gluing them in place.

Grandparent's Day Vase Pattern

HAPPY BIRTHDAY CELEBRATIONS

You need:
• glue
• oaktag
• scissors
• crayons or markers
• glitter
• stapler
Optional: bobby pins

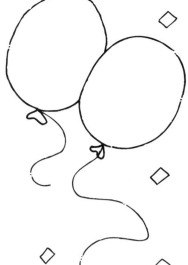

1. Reproduce the crown pattern on page 20 twice and glue it onto oaktag.
   Cut out and let the birthday child decorate it. Staple to fit so that the
   birthday child can wear it during the day. (If needed, use bobby pins to
   more securely attach the crown.)
2. Reproduce the cake patterns on pages 21 and 22. Cut out and glue together,
   as shown.
3. On the birthday cake, ask the birthday child to write or dictate a sentence about something important
   he or she has done during the past year. Then ask the child to write or dictate a sentence about
   something he or she would like to do in the upcoming year.
4. Reserve a corner of the room or a part of the bulletin board to display a sample of the birthday
   child's work. Include the birthday cake from Step 3, as well as special pictures of family or other
   mementos from home. Leave the birthday cake up for several days.
5. Encourage children whose birthdays fall on the weekend to celebrate their birthdays at school
   on a Friday or a Monday. For summer birthdays, reserve a day or two during the last week of school
   to celebrate.

BIRTHDAY CAKE BULLETIN BOARD

You need:
• crayons or markers
• clear contact paper
• scissors
• pushpins or tape
• oaktag

1. Reproduce the cake patterns on pages 21 and 22. Color, laminate, and cut out.
2. Assemble the layers of cake on a wall or bulletin board, as shown.
3. Reproduce the candle pattern on page 20 and cut out. Trace the candle on oaktag once for each child.
4. Have children decorate their candles. Label each candle with the child's name and birthday.
5. On the first day of each month, attach the birthday candles for that month to the cake. Add a banner above the cake that indicates the current month (for example, "January Birthdays") as shown.

Birthday Crown and Candle Pattern

HAPPY BIRTHDAY TO ME!

Bottom Layer of Cake Pattern

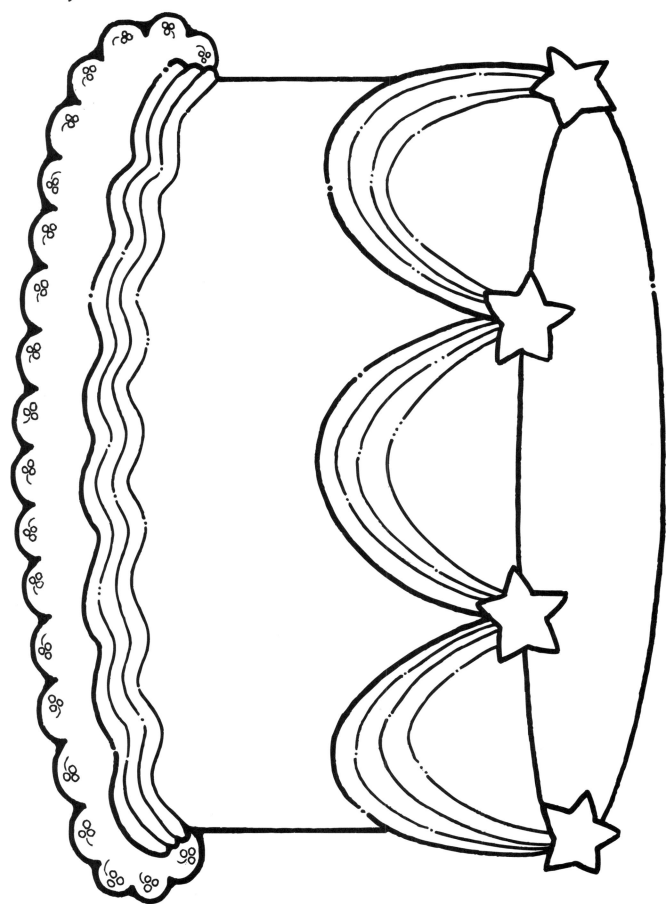

Top Layer of Cake Pattern

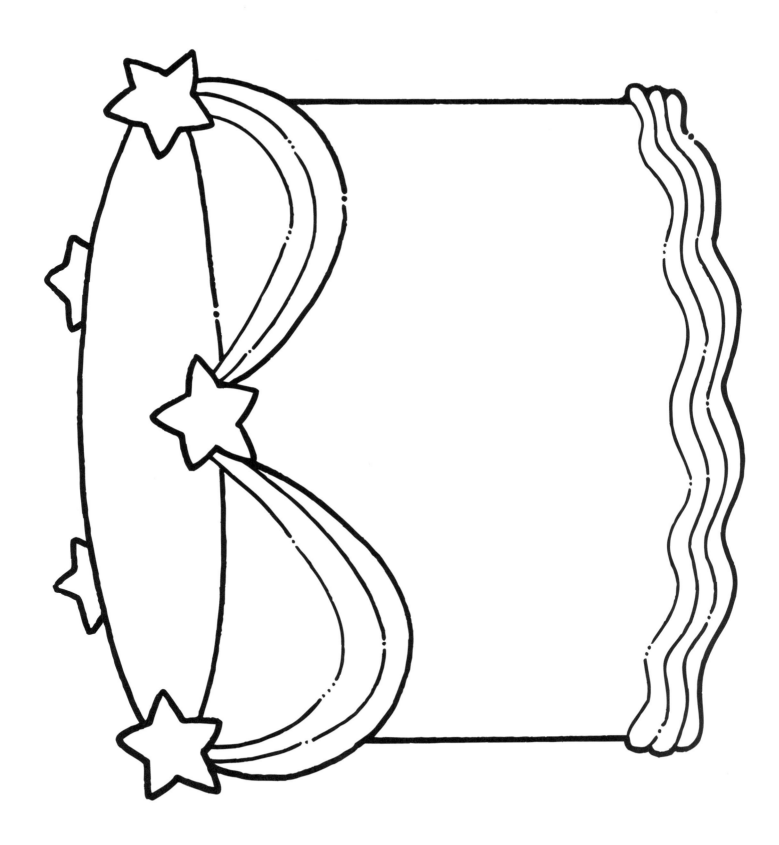

Name _____

Circle the five birthday words hidden in the puzzle below. Color the picture. Then turn the page over and draw your own picture of a birthday celebration.

HAPPY   BIRTHDAY   CANDLE   GIFT   CAKE

R	B	I	R	T	H	D	A	Y	K
X	Z	U	D	J	G	I	F	T	C
C	A	K	E	F	Q	P	W	X	T
G	M	H	A	P	P	Y	W	Z	M
V	Q	R	H	C	A	N	D	L	E

Newbridge

BIRTHDAY CAKE CARD

You need:
• 12" x 18" construction paper
• stapler
• scissors
• magazines
• glue
• crayons or markers

1. Reproduce the cake patterns on pages 21 and 22. Glue the layers together on a 12" x 18" piece of construction paper, as shown.
2. Take another piece of construction paper and staple together, as shown, to make a giant card.
3. During free time, children can cut out small pictures from old magazines or draw pictures of presents they would like to give the birthday child.
4. Each child can glue one present on the inside of the card and sign his or her name.
5. After everyone has decorated and signed the card, the birthday child may take the card home.

Steps 1 and 2

Step 4

CLASSROOM HELPER TRAIN

You need:
- crayons or markers
- clear contact paper
- scissors
- permanent marker
- pushpins or tape
- yarn
- 4" x 24" strip of construction paper
- index cards
- envelope

1. Reproduce the engine and caboose patterns on pages 27 and 29. Color, laminate, and cut out.
2. Reproduce the middle car pattern on page 28 as many times as there are classroom duties. Color, laminate, and cut out.
3. On each of the middle cars, write a classroom job. (Permanent marker can be used to write on laminated materials.) Review the responsibilities of each job with the class. Job possibilities include: line leader, calendar helper, snack monitor, paper monitor, errand runner, animal keeper, and so on.
4. Attach the helper train to a wall or bulletin board. Use yarn to connect the cars, as shown.
5. Write "Classroom Helpers" on a 4" x 24" strip of construction paper and attach it to the wall or bulletin board above the train.
6. Give each child an index card. Ask children to write their names on their cards and decorate them.
7. Collect all the cards and store them in an envelope. Each day (or each week, if preferred) draw out the number of cards needed to perform all jobs, making sure that each child has an opportunity to learn how to do each job. Tape the index cards to each of the helper train cars, as shown.

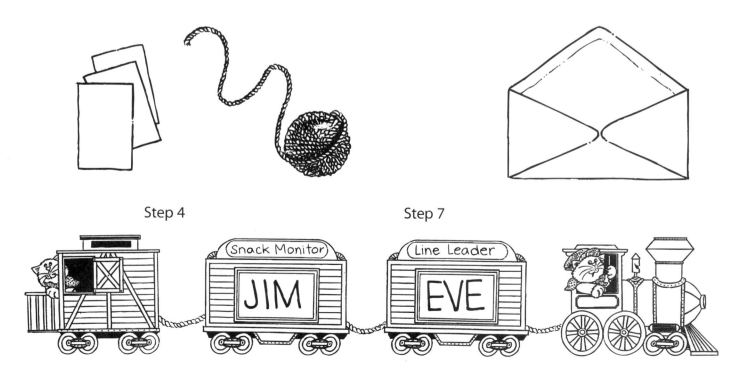

Step 4   Step 7

STORYTIME TRAIN

You need:
- oaktag
- glue
- crayons or markers
- scissors
- six shoe boxes (without covers)
- hole puncher
- yarn
- small dolls, stuffed animals, magazines

1. Reproduce the engine and caboose patterns on pages 27 and 29. Mount on oaktag, color, and cut out.
2. Reproduce the middle car pattern on page 28 four times. Mount on oaktag, color, and cut out.
3. Glue the engine pattern on one side of a shoe box, as shown. Repeat with the caboose and middle cars on five more shoe boxes.
4. Punch holes in the back of the engine shoe box and the front of the caboose shoe box. Punch holes in the front and back of the middle car shoe boxes.
5. Thread yarn through the holes, as shown, to attach the cars of the train.
6. Encourage small groups or individuals to reenact the story of *The Little Engine That Could* using small dolls, stuffed animals, pictures clipped from magazines, and so on.
7. For variation, children may use train cars for sorting games. Give children objects that can be sorted by colors, number, shape, or size.

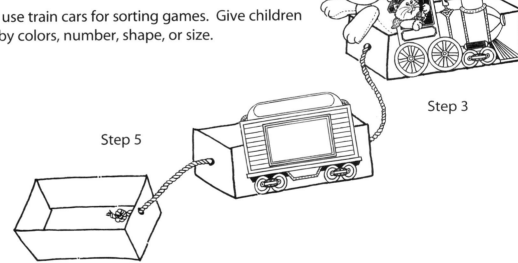

Step 3

Step 5

RECOMMENDED READING

Read the following storybooks to your class. Place the books on a reading table or in a bookcase so that the children may look at them during free time.

All Aboard the Train by Ethel and Leonard Kessler, published by Doubleday.
Choo Choo by Virginia Lee Burton, published by Houghton Mifflin.
Trains by Anne Rockwell, published by Dutton.
Train Song by Diane Siebert, published by HarperCollins.
Two Little Trains by Margaret Wise Brown, published by Addison Wesley.

Engine Pattern

Middle Car Pattern

Caboose Pattern

FOLLOW THE TRAIN

Follow the path that each train is taking. Use a different-colored crayon to show each path.

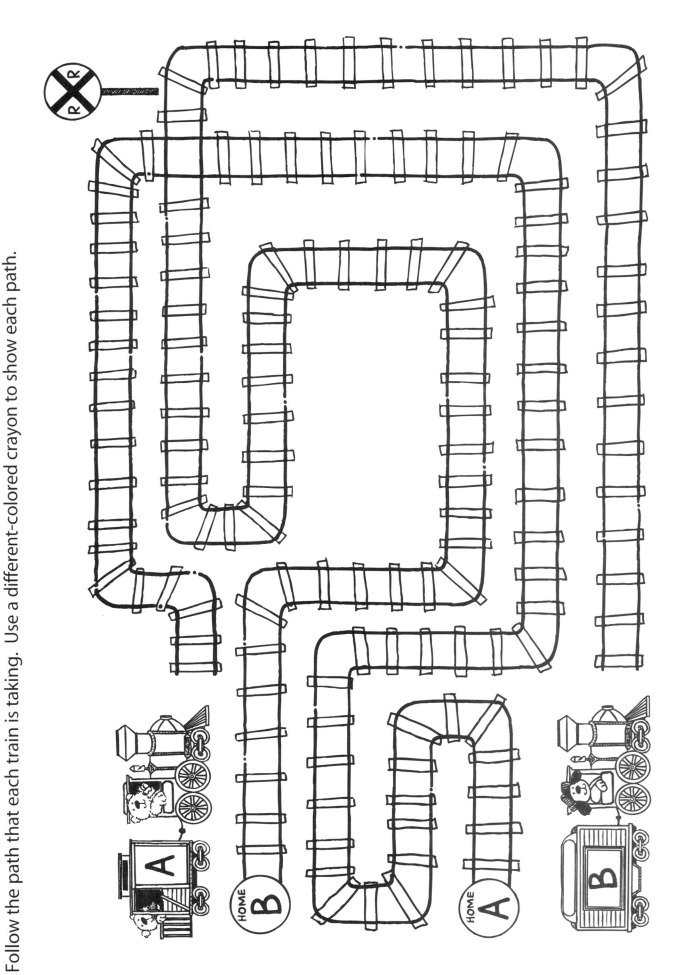

Newbridge

MOUSE PAPER-BAG PUPPETS

You need:
• crayons or markers
• scissors
• glue
• brown paper lunch bags

1. Ask each child to choose one of the mouse body patterns on pages 33 and 34 to make a paper-bag puppet. Reproduce the mouse head pattern on page 32 and the selected body pattern for each child. Have children color and cut out.
2. Have each child glue the head to the bottom of a brown paper lunch bag. Then have each child glue the mouse body to the front of the lunch bag so the head overlaps the neck, as shown.
3. For activities, see Cat and Mouse Game on page 35 and Five Little Mice Action Poem on page 36.

Mouse Head Pattern

Mouse Body Pattern

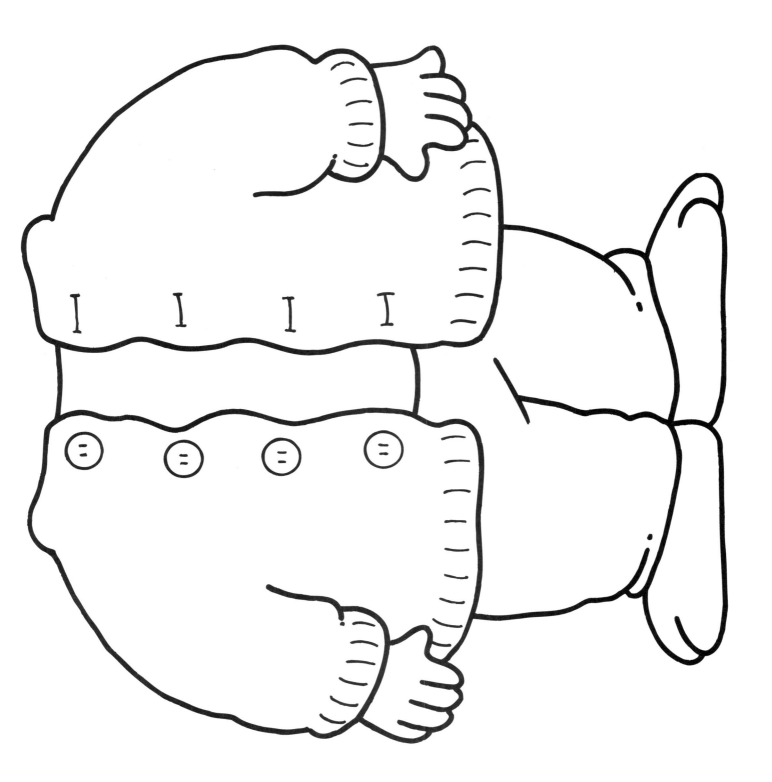

Mouse Body Pattern

IF YOU GIVE A MOUSE A COOKIE CLASS BOOK

Read the book *If You Give a Mouse a Cookie* (by Laura J. Numeroff, published by HarperCollins) to the class. Discuss with children how the mouse is not satisfied with what he gets. Ask children why they think the mouse always wants something more. Then make the following class book.

1. Reproduce the mouse head pattern on page 32 and a body pattern on pages 33 or 34 for each child. Have children color and cut out.
2. Have each child tape the mouse head and body together.
3. Help each child tape together two pieces of 12" x 18" construction paper along the 18" side. Then have the children glue their mice onto the paper.
4. Tell children to draw speech bubbles coming out of the mice's mouths. Have each child write or dictate a sentence that describes something the mouse might want.
5. Tape two blank pieces of 12" x 18" construction paper together to make a cover. Write the title "If You Give a Mouse a Cookie Class Book" on the cover.
6. Stack the pages with the cover on top and punch two holes on the left side. Thread a piece of yarn through each hole and tie into a bow, as shown.

CAT AND MOUSE GAME

1. Explain the meaning of the saying "When the cat's away the mice will play" to the class. Then choose one child to be the cat. Tell the rest of the class to hold up their paper-bag puppets so they can be the mice.
2. Have the cat stand in the middle of the playing floor with mice lined up to the right and left of him or her.
3. When you call "The cat's away," the mice must run from their side to the opposite side.
4. The cat should try to catch the mice by tagging the puppets. If the cat catches a mouse, that child is the next cat. If the cat does not catch a mouse, he or she must try one more time before a new cat is picked.

FIVE LITTLE MICE
ACTION POEM

Five little mice
Running here and there.
Then they saw a cat
And had an awful scare.
Quietly they ran
Underneath the stair,
And when it was time to play again,
Only four would dare.

Four little mice…

Three little mice…

Two little mice…

One little mouse
Running here and there.
Then s/he saw a cat
And had an awful scare.
Quietly s/he ran
Underneath the stair,
And when it was time to play again,
None of them would dare.

ALPHABET TRAIL FILE-FOLDER GAME

You need:
- crayons or markers
- oaktag
- glue
- letter-sized file folder
- clear contact paper
- scissors
- stapler
- envelope
- four different-colored buttons for playing pieces
- die

1. Reproduce the game board on pages 40 and 41 and the how-to-play directions on page 38 once. Reproduce the game cards on page 39 twice. Color the game board and game cards.
2. Glue the game board on the inside of a letter-sized file folder. Glue the how-to-play directions on the front of the folder. Laminate both sides of the folder.
3. Mount the game cards on oaktag. Laminate and cut out.
4. Staple an envelope to the back of the folder. Store the game cards, a die, and four different-colored buttons in the envelope.

ALPHABET TRAIL FILE-FOLDER GAME INSTRUCTIONS

HOW TO PLAY
(for 2 to 4 players)

1. Each player chooses a playing piece.
2. One player shuffles the cards and puts them near the game board.
3. The youngest player goes first and draws a card from the pile. The player then moves to the alphabet letter space that matches the beginning sound of the object shown on the card.
4. After moving, the player returns the card to the bottom of the card pile and the next player takes a turn.
5. The first player to reach the Alphabet Clubhouse becomes president of the Alphabet Club.
6. Players may continue the game until all the players reach the Alphabet Clubhouse.

Alphabet Trail Game Cards

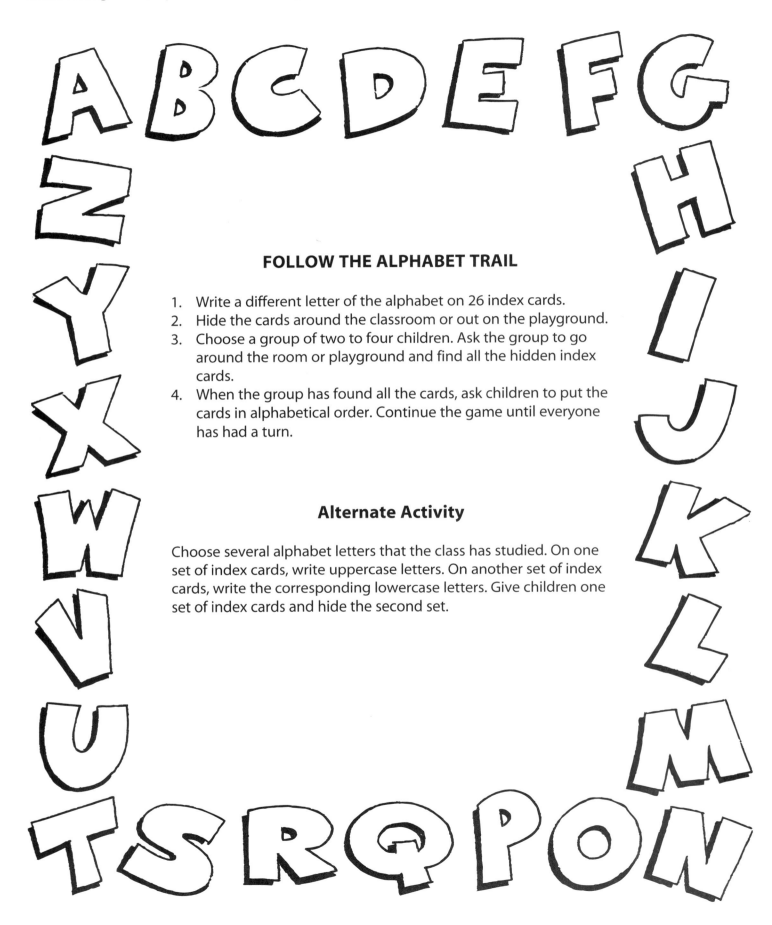

FOLLOW THE ALPHABET TRAIL

1. Write a different letter of the alphabet on 26 index cards.
2. Hide the cards around the classroom or out on the playground.
3. Choose a group of two to four children. Ask the group to go around the room or playground and find all the hidden index cards.
4. When the group has found all the cards, ask children to put the cards in alphabetical order. Continue the game until everyone has had a turn.

Alternate Activity

Choose several alphabet letters that the class has studied. On one set of index cards, write uppercase letters. On another set of index cards, write the corresponding lowercase letters. Give children one set of index cards and hide the second set.

ALPHABET TRAIL SCAVENGER HUNT

1. Divide the class into pairs, giving each pair an index card with an alphabet letter printed on it.
2. Give children five minutes to look for objects in the room that begin with the same letter as the letter on the cards.
3. Have the pairs of children point out the objects to the rest of the class.

ALPHABET CLUB RIDDLES

1. Tell children they are part of a class alphabet club. The rules of membership in the club are that they must answer alphabet riddles.
2. Describe several objects around the room. (The objects may all be limited to one particular alphabet letter, or they may be distributed throughout the alphabet.)
3. Begin each description with the object's sound. Then add a couple of clues describing properties of the object.
4. Tell children to look around the room to solve the riddles. If no one can guess the answer to the riddle, give the class more clues.
5. After children are familiar with the game, use the game cards to play. Ask one child to choose a game card and then describe the object on the card by giving its beginning sound and a couple of clues about the object.
6. The first child who guesses correctly becomes the next person who gives the clues.

ALPHABET CLUB GAME

You need:
• crayons or markers
• glue
• oaktag
• scissors
• hole puncher
• 24" lengths of yarn

1. Reproduce the badge pattern on this page for each child. Have children color the badges, mount on oaktag, and cut out.
2. Help each child punch a hole at the top of the badge where indicated.
3. Give each child a 24" length of yarn. Help children thread the yarn through the holes and tie together.
4. Children may wear their badges while playing Alphabet Trail Scavenger Hunt and Alphabet Club Riddles.

HIDDEN ALPHABET

Find the eight alphabet letters hidden in the classroom.
Then color the picture.

44

Newbridge

WORD ROUNDUP BULLETIN BOARD

You need:
• crayons or markers
• scissors
• tape
• glue
• oaktag
• light brown construction paper
• yarn
• stapler
• craft sticks
Optional: clear construction paper

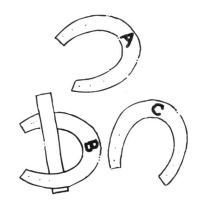

1. Reproduce the patterns on pages 46 through 48 once. Color the cat and mouse and cut out. Tape the cat together, as shown, and mount both figures on oaktag. Laminate if desired.
2. Cut out the horseshoe pattern. Trace it onto a piece of oaktag several times and cut out. Give the oaktag horseshoes to children to trace onto light brown construction paper.
3. Have each child take and cut out one horseshoe. Collect the horseshoes. On each horseshoe, write a word that the class has recently learned, a decodable word, or a familiar sight word.
4. Draw a large lasso shape with glue on construction paper. Lay a piece of yarn over the glue and let dry. Staple the lasso to one side of the bulletin board.
5. Staple the cat to the bulletin board so that it appears to be holding the lasso, as shown.
6. Staple the mouse to the other side of the bulletin board. Use brown construction paper to make a pole for the horseshoes to ring.
7. Place the horseshoes on and around the pole, as shown.
8. Title the bulletin board "Word Roundup" by writing out the words in glue inside the lasso and then placing pieces of yarn over the glue.
9. Attach craft sticks around the edges of the bulletin board to form a corral-type border, as shown.
10. For younger children, title the bulletin board "ABC Roundup" and print a letter of the alphabet on each horseshoe.

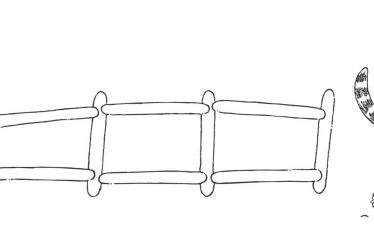

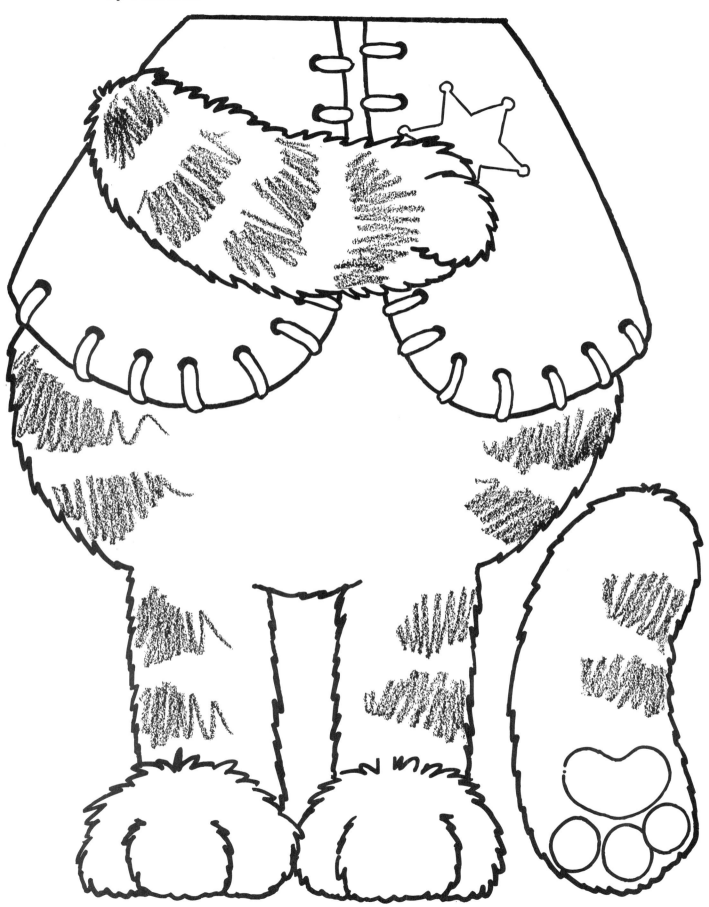

HORSESHOE TOSS

1. Reproduce the horseshoe pattern on page 48 twenty-one times and cut out.
2. Mount one horseshoe on cardboard. Color and cut out.
3. On the remaining horseshoes, draw different numbers of dots from 1 to 20.
4. Spread the horseshoes out on the floor, as shown.
5. Ask for a volunteer to "toss" the cardboard horseshoe so that it lands on or near one of the horseshoes on the floor. Then ask the child to count the dots on the horseshoe and tell the class the answer.
6. Remove that horseshoe from the floor. Then give the cardboard horseshoe to another child. Continue playing until everyone has had a turn.
7. For older children, write simple addition and subtraction equations on each horseshoe instead of drawing dots. Or, write a numeral from 1 to 20 on each horseshoe. Then ask each child to tell you if a random numeral is greater or less than the number he or she has tossed the cardboard horseshoe upon.

COWBOY COUNTRY

Look carefully at the picture. Then follow the directions below.

1. Color the prairie dog brown.
2. Put a circle around the cowboy's boots.
3. Color the cowboy's saddle blue
4. Color his bandana red.
5. Draw a fence around the cattle.

COWBOY CAMPING DRAMATIC PLAY CENTER

Before setting up this dramatic play center, have a class discussion about cowboys. Ask volunteers to tell some things they know about what cowboys did. Then read the book *Cowboy Small* by Lois Lenski, published by McKay, to the class.

You need:
• 6' to 8' length of clothesline or rope
• light blanket or sheet
• books
• children's cowboy hats
• bandanas
• hobbyhorses

1. Stretch a 6' to 8' length of clothesline or rope across a small corner of the room, anchoring it from one piece of furniture to another.
2. Drape an old blanket or a sheet over the rope. Pull the edges of the drape and anchor them with books, forming a tent shape.
3. Place cowboy hats, bandanas, and hobbyhorses around the tent.
4. Children can ride on the hobbyhorses, sleep in the tent, and wear hats and bandanas as they pretend to be cowboys and cowgirls.
5. Children may also wish to sing songs such as "Home on the Range" while playing in the dramatic play center.

JOHNNY APPLESEED FLANNEL BOARD STORY

This is the story of Johnny Appleseed, whose real name was John Chapman. When John Chapman was born in 1775, America was very different from the way it is today. In fact, our country was not yet called the United States. Most of the settlers in the New World lived along the East Coast. Johnny lived among the rolling hills and green fields of Pennsylvania. One day he watched a group of people pack up covered wagons and begin to travel west. To the west were wilderness lands filled with forests and animals. Every time Johnny watched a covered wagon go by, he was filled with a longing to go west too. "I know what to do!" said Johnny as he munched an apple. "I've heard there aren't any apple trees growing in the wilderness. Maybe I can bring apples to the new settlers."

Johnny packed a sack full of apple saplings and seeds, a few clothes, a pot for cooking, and off he went. He floated down the Ohio River in a canoe, he hiked through forests, he ate wild berries and plants, and he slept under the stars. Sometimes it rained, but Johnny never minded. He just put his old cooking pot on his head to keep the rain off. He often walked for days without seeing a single person, but he was never lonely. The animals knew he would not hurt them, so they walked right up to him and kept him company.

Johnny visited many Indian villages. From the Indians he learned a great deal about using plants and herbs to make medicine for sick people. When Johnny saw a settler's cabin, he knew he could look forward to a few days of good meals and good company. The settlers were always happy to see him, and best of all, Johnny had a chance to share his apples with new friends. Johnny planted tiny apple trees all over the settlers' land, told wonderful stories, brought news from cabin to cabin, and showed the settlers how to make medicine using plants and herbs, like the Indians had taught him.

For forty years Johnny traveled around, visiting settlers and planting apple trees. His name became well known in the lands we now call Illinois, Ohio, and Indiana. Folks began to call him Johnny Appleseed. Johnny was filled with happiness as he watched the tiny trees he had planted become bigger and bigger. He loved to pick apples and carefully saved all the seeds. Then he planted some of the seeds and saved some for new settlers. The dream that Johnny Appleseed had as a young man had come true. He really did bring apples to the settlers in the West. And people today still remember him for his good work.

JOHNNY APPLESEED FLANNEL BOARD

You need:
• scissors
• flannel
• crayons or markers
• glue
Optional: 1/2" x 1/2" sandpaper squares

1. Reproduce the patterns on pages 54 through 56 once and cut out.
2. Trace the figures on scraps of flannel and cut out, or color the paper figures and glue small pieces of flannel or sandpaper squares to the backs, as shown.
3. Move the figures around the flannel board as you read the story of Johnny Appleseed on page 52 to the class.
4. Later, place the flannel board and figures where children can reach them. Let children retell the story or make up new adventures for Johnny Appleseed.

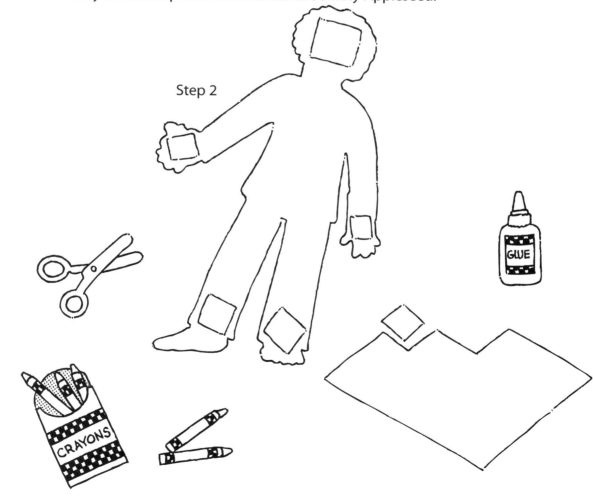

Step 2

Johnny Appleseed Patterns

APPLE SEEDS

Johnny Appleseed Patterns

Johnny Appleseed Patterns

APPLE TREE SEQUENCING

Name _____

Color the pictures of Johnny Appleseed and his trees.
Cut the pictures apart. Then glue them on another
sheet of paper in the correct order.

APPLE TREE RHYME

You need:
• scissors
• crayons or markers

1. Reproduce the apple tree pattern on page 55 as many times as there are children in the class and cut out. On the trunk of each tree, write a numeral from 1 to 10.
2. Give each child a tree. Have each child draw the number of apples on the tree that corresponds to the numeral written on the trunk. Then ask children to color in the apples and trees.
3. Recite the action rhyme below, varying the number of apples from one to ten with each verse.
4. Ask children who have the corresponding number of apples on their trees as featured in the verse to stand up and be the leaders when that verse is being recited.

Way up high in an apple tree,
(hold arms over head)

Two little apples smiled at me.
(hold up two fingers to cheeks)

I shook that tree as hard as I could.
(pretend to shake tree)

Down came two apples. Mmmm, they were good!
(rub stomach and smile)

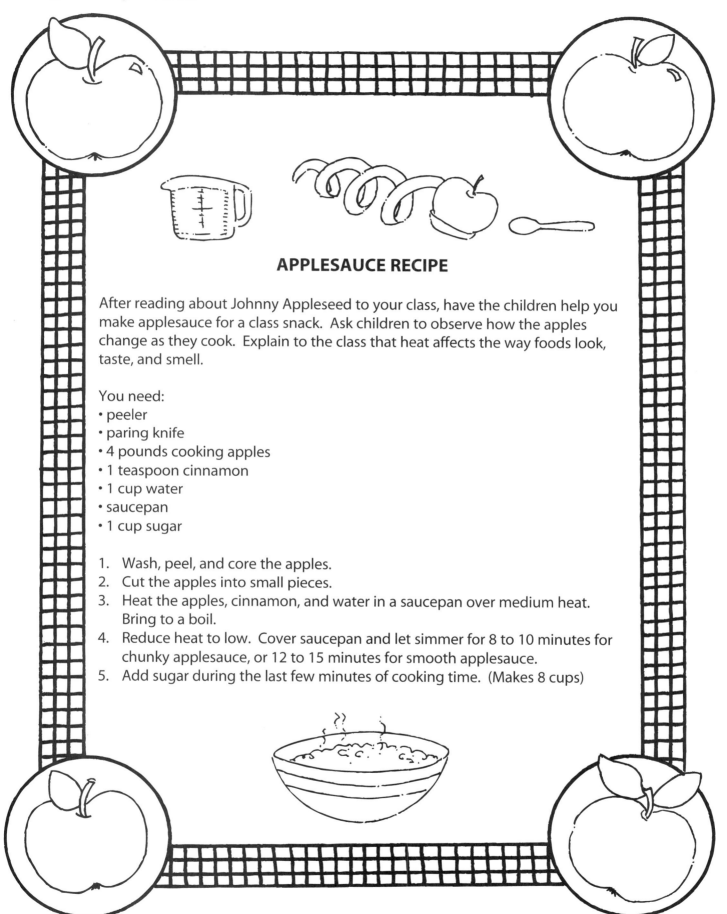

APPLESAUCE RECIPE

After reading about Johnny Appleseed to your class, have the children help you make applesauce for a class snack. Ask children to observe how the apples change as they cook. Explain to the class that heat affects the way foods look, taste, and smell.

You need:
- peeler
- paring knife
- 4 pounds cooking apples
- 1 teaspoon cinnamon
- 1 cup water
- saucepan
- 1 cup sugar

1. Wash, peel, and core the apples.
2. Cut the apples into small pieces.
3. Heat the apples, cinnamon, and water in a saucepan over medium heat. Bring to a boil.
4. Reduce heat to low. Cover saucepan and let simmer for 8 to 10 minutes for chunky applesauce, or 12 to 15 minutes for smooth applesauce.
5. Add sugar during the last few minutes of cooking time. (Makes 8 cups)

COMMUNITY HELPERS HAND PUPPETS

You need:
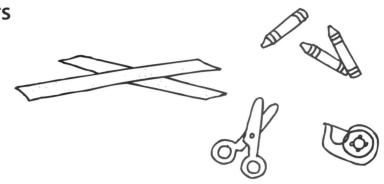
• crayons or markers
• scissors
• 1" x 6" strips of oaktag
• stapler
• tape
• glue

1. Reproduce the community helpers patterns on pages 61 through 63 for each child. Have children color and cut out.
2. Give each child six 1" x 6" strips of oaktag. Show children how to loop the strips around their hands. Staple each loop closed to fit around each child's hand, as shown.
3. Demonstrate how to staple the patterns onto the loops. Show children how to wear the hand puppets so that they face out from the palm of their hands.
4. Ask each child to place a particular worker on his or her hand and name it, then describe what that worker's job entails.
5. Discuss with the class what might happen if those workers did not come in to work. How would people get rid of their garbage? What might happen to people who are sick? What might happen if someone needed the police and they were not there?
6. Survey children to find out who might want to become a community helper when he or she grows up and why.

Step 2

Step 3

US
MAIL

COMMUNITY HELPERS ACCORDION BOOK

1. Reproduce the helpers patterns on pages 61 through 63 for each child. Have children color and cut out.
2. Give each child a piece of 12" x 18" construction paper and demonstrate how to fold the paper. Tell children to fold the paper in half widthwise, then fold the top half back toward the fold, as shown. Turn the paper over and fold that half back as well. Turn the book over again so the cover page opens to the left.
3. Since these books will accommodate only four community workers pictures, children must fold an extra sheet and cut in half, then tape to the end of the books, as shown. Now each book can feature six workers.
4. Help children glue one worker in the middle of each page. Above each worker, help children write the name of the worker. Under each worker, have children write or dictate a few sentences about the work he or she does.
5. Lastly, allow time for children to design a cover for their books. Children may wish to read their books to the class and share what they have done.

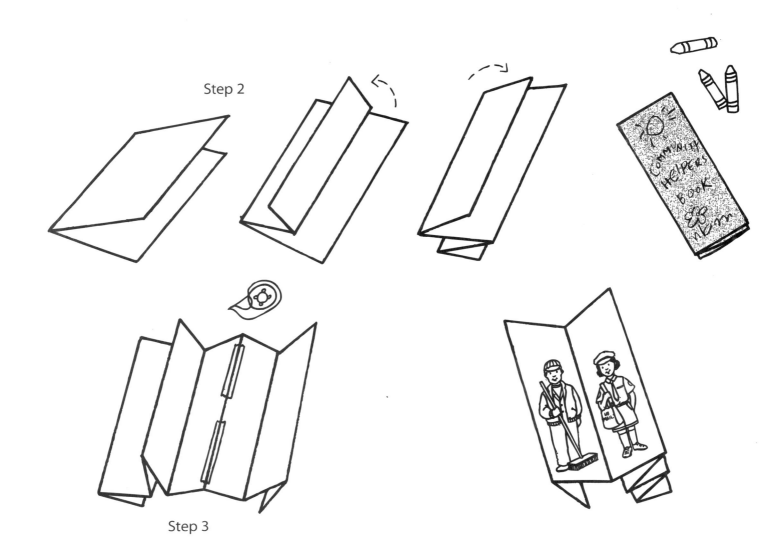

Step 2

Step 3

NEIGHBORHOOD WALK

1. Collect pictures and books about community workers. Share them with the class, helping children to identify each worker and the equipment with which the workers perform their jobs. Ask children to describe the uniforms and clothing worn by certain community helpers and why they think that particular form of clothing is appropriate.
2. Ask children to identify what they would like to be when they grow up. Write children's comments on chart paper. Encourage them to tell why they wish to be in a certain line of work.
3. Have each child draw a picture about his or her chosen job, showing the type of work that person does, the clothes he or she wears, equipment he or she uses, or the place most associated with that kind of work.
4. Bind children's papers into a class book, or display separately on a wall or bulletin board with children's writing or dictation about their future careers.

COMMUNITY HELPERS RECOMMENDED READING

Read the following books about community helpers to the class. Place the books on a reading table or in a bookcase so that children may look at them during free time.

An Auto Mechanic by Douglas Florian, published by William Morrow.
Doctor De Soto by William Steig, published by Farrar, Straus & Giroux.
Fire! Fire! by Gail Gibbons, published by HarperCollins.
A Visit to the Police Station by Dotti Hannum, published by Children's Press.
We're Taking an Airplane Trip by Dinah Moche, published by Western Publishing Company.

DAY AND NIGHT BULLETIN BOARD

You need:
• crayons or markers
• glue
• oaktag
• scissors
• stapler
• light blue and black bulletin board paper
• two brown paper grocery bags
• construction paper
• aluminum foil
Optional: clear contact paper

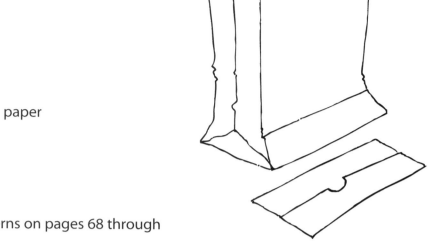

1. Reproduce all the animal patterns on pages 68 through 70 once.
2. Color the figures, mount on oaktag, and cut out. Laminate if desired.
3. Divide the bulletin board in half. On the left side attach light blue background paper, and on the right side attach black background paper.
4. Label the blue side of the bulletin board "Day" and the black side "Night."
5. Cut off the bottoms of two brown paper grocery bags. Cut along one side of each bag and then flatten it into one long piece.
6. From each bag cut one long, wide strip to make a tree trunk and one or two shorter, thinner strips to make branches. Crumple the paper and smooth it out again.
7. Attach one tree trunk and branches to the day side of the bulletin board, and one tree trunk and branches to the night side.
8. Attach the day animals on and around the day tree, and the night animals on and around the night tree.
9. Have children use construction paper to make buildings and houses. Attach the buildings to both sides of the bulletin board. Tell children to color the windows in the night buildings yellow.
10. Ask children to make leaves for the trees out of construction paper.
11. Have children make a moon and stars out of aluminum foil. Attach them to the night side of the bulletin board.
12. Have the class draw people on both sides of the bulletin board.
13. For activities, see Day and Night Words on page 71 and Day and Night Class Discussion on page 72.

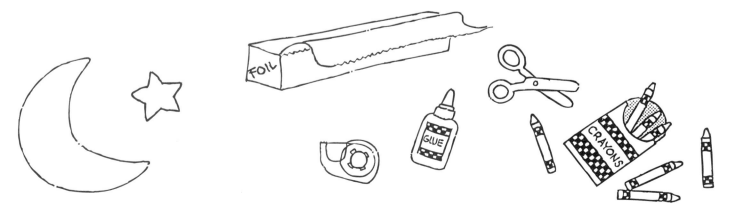

Animal Patterns

Animal Patterns

DAY AND NIGHT WORDS

You need:
• crayons and markers
• oaktag
• pushpins or tacks
• construction paper
• scissors
• glue

1. Draw a line down the middle of a piece of oaktag to make two columns. Label one column "Day" and the other "Night."
2. Ask volunteers to think of words that are associated with day. Make a list of the words under the day heading. Have children think of words associated with night, and make another list under the night heading.
3. Attach the list to the Day and Night Bulletin Board.
4. As an extension activity, have children choose a pattern from pages 68 through 70 and cut out. Have children glue the pattern on a piece of construction paper and draw a scene involving the animal. Encourage children to write or dictate stories about day and night animals.

DAY AND NIGHT CLASS DISCUSSION

1. Ask volunteers to name some similarities and differences between day and night. Explain to the class that day and night occur all over the world—and on other planets, too.
2. Ask children if they know anyone who works at night. Talk about various night workers, such as workers in restaurants, stores, police and fire stations; bus and truck drivers; construction workers; and so on. Explain to the class that it is very important that many people work through the night because sometimes people need emergency medical care, or people need transportation, and so on. Compare night workers with day workers. When do night workers sleep? How are their lives different from those of people who work during the day?
3. Tell children that Labor Day is a special holiday that honors working people. Discuss the fact that many businesses and public service facilities are open 24 hours a day.
4. Compare day animals with nocturnal animals. Tell children that *nocturnal* means these animals are active at night. Point out that nocturnal animals have good night vision. Explain why it is more important for these animals to "work" at night rather than during the day.
5. Ask children to draw pictures of people who work during the day and people who work at night. Attach the pictures next to the Day and Night Bulletin Board.

Day and Night are opposites. Draw lines to match the pictures on the left with their opposites on the right.

BACK-TO-SCHOOL DINOSAUR PUZZLES

HOW TO PLAY:

1. Reproduce the dinosaur pattern on page 75 for each child.
2. Have children color, cut out, and laminate their dinosaur patterns.
3. Help each child write his or her name on the dinosaur's book bag.
4. Show children how to cut the pattern into four or five pieces to make a puzzle, as shown.
5. Encourage children to practice putting together and taking apart their puzzles as quickly as they can.
6. Extend the activity by pairing up the students and inviting them to do each other's name puzzles.

Dinosaur Pattern

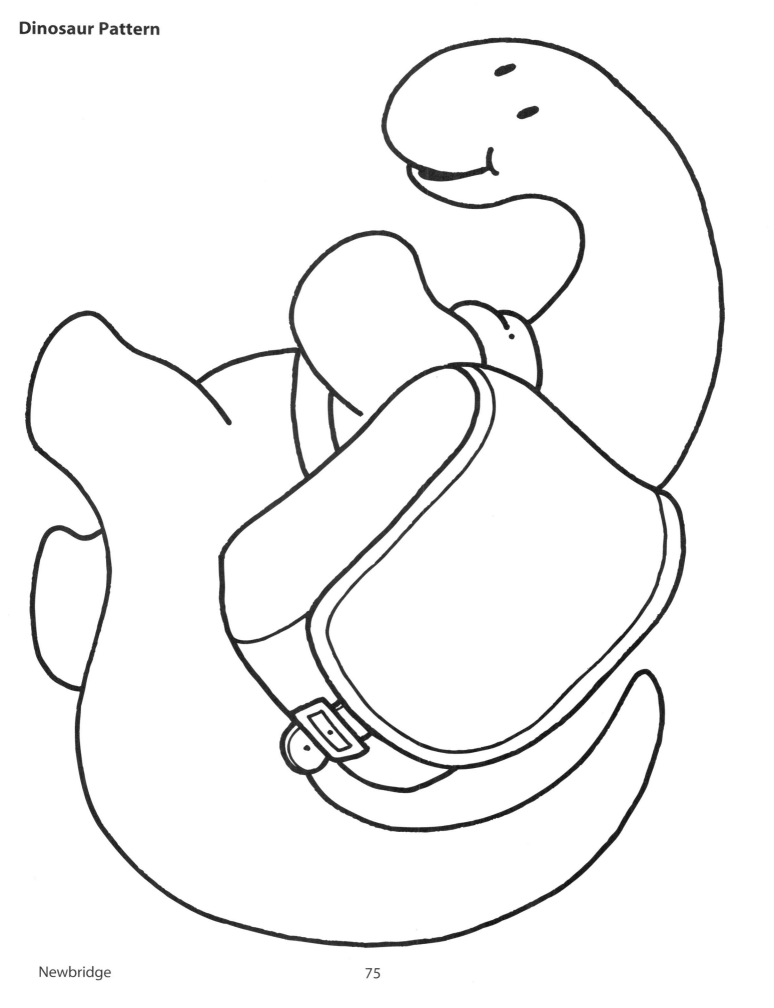

CRAYON TWISTER

HOW TO PLAY:

1. Reproduce the crayon pattern on page 77 twelve times. Have children color and cut out.
2. Glue each crayon onto a small piece of oaktag.
3. Help children tape or paste the twelve crayon patterns to the floor in a gridlike pattern, sorting by colors as shown.
4. Organize the class into small groups. Have a volunteer start the game.
5. Either make a simple color-coded spinner out of oaktag and a brass fastener for the children to spin, or write the directions on the board for each round. For example: "Right hand on yellow crayon" or "Left hand on green crayon."
6. Gradually invite the other children to join in. Continue the game until the children can twist their bodies no further or lose their balance.

Crayon Pattern

THE SAFETY GAME

HOW TO PLAY:

1. Reproduce the bus pattern on page 79 several times. Write bus numbers on the sides, as shown. Staple the buses to the bulletin board.
2. Organize children by the number of the bus they ride each day.
3. Call out a bus number and ask that particular group to think of a safety tip. Ask a volunteer from the group to come up and recite the safety tip to the rest of the class. On the chalkboard, record the group's safety tip. Continue until all the groups have participated.
4. Help the groups write their different safety tips on the bus patterns. Display the buses around the classroom. They will serve both as reminders of important safety tips and the children's bus numbers.

School Bus Pattern

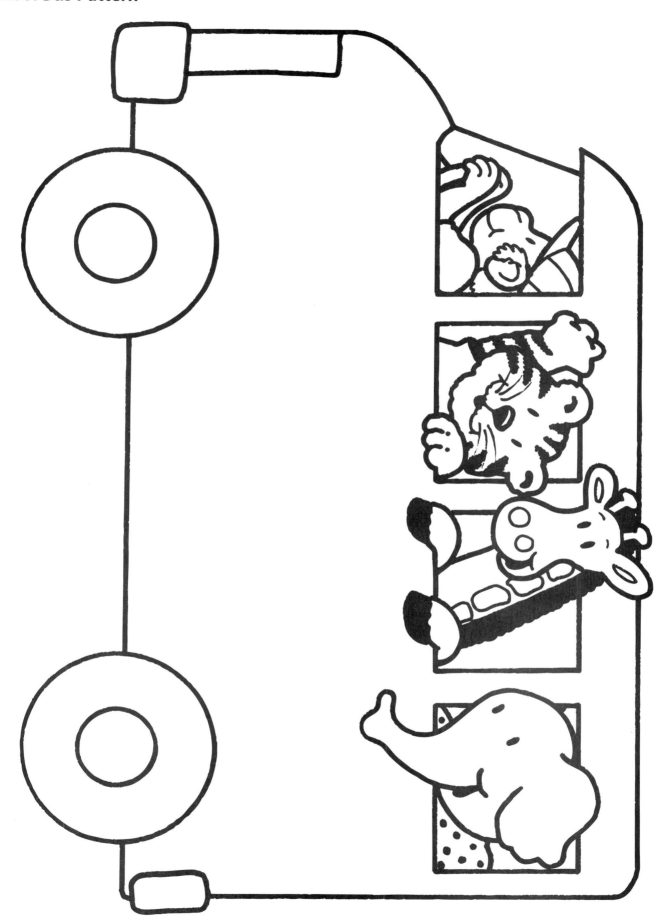

Teacher's Notes